Would'st thou divert thyself from melancholy?

John Bunyan, *Pilgrim's Progress*, 1678

To the memory of my grandmother, Josephine Mazur, whose long pilgrimage—undertaken in faith and with such a spirit of true grace that I doubt whether I will ever witness the like again—was such an inspiration to her family. To her great-granddaughter Avery Smith, whose pilgrimage just began as these words were being assembled herein.

And to those pilgrims whose words of optimism, encouragement, and wonder recorded in these pages help reveal to us the true Way: pilgrimage as a process, not a product.

CONTENTS

FOREWORD

Reading this book is itself a pilgrimage. Reading it as a tourist will not do. One must bring one's heart to it. But that is not difficult to do for the words and images elicit the heart and get under the skin of self consciousness and comfort that so smother the soul in the busy lives many of us live today. The passages take one into solitude and quiet as well as into great bliss and moments of connectedness—into the "via negativa" and the "via positiva" that the mystics speak of.

The pilgrims in these pages talk about their physical hardships—blisters and tiredness, exhaustion and very sore feet. But they keep going. They speak of how physical pain can lead one into Spirit, not away from it. They are speaking from their experience, not from something they read in a book. All mysticism is about return to experience. It is about tasting, as the psalmist sings of when he says: "Taste and see that God is good." No one can taste for us. No one can walk for another person. We do our own walking. Our own hurting. Our own observing and connecting. These pages demonstrate this with depth and honesty.

On reading the reflections in this book I was reminded of a friend of mine who walked, with his dog, across the

United States from Washington D.C. to Los Angeles a num-
ber of years ago. It was something he had always wanted to
do. The day they arrived in Los Angeles the Watts riots
erupted—and they walked right into it. He said he might
make the cross-country journey again some day, the whole
experience was so exhilarating. His dog has since passed on.

I was also reminded of hearing the daughter of Rabbi
Abraham Heschel tell the story of how her father had
marched in Selma with Dr. Martin Luther King Jr. and when
he returned home she, a child of about ten, asked her father
what it was like: "I felt my feet were praying," he said. Many
of the pilgrims speaking herein of their journey might have
borrowed that line from Heschel: feet pray. If we let them.

I am reminded of retreats with Thich Naht Hahn who
also instructs us to be conscious of our feet praying, to be
fully present to our feet, to the now, and not walk *to get
some place* but... to walk. As Meiset Eckhart says, to "work
without a why, to "work for the sake of working." We
might add: To walk for the sake of walking.

While we still have feet, we ought to walk. While we
still have eyes, we ought to observe. While we still have
ears, we ought to listen. While we have existence on this
earth, we ought to be fully present here. These are lessons
that they mystics teach and they are lessons that come
through clearly in the pages of this book. It is living in
what Eckhart calls the "eternal now." It is our way of
saying "Thank You" for having feet, eyes, ears, existence
and the holy earth. It is holy gratitude.

All these teachings about living in the now, about

being fully present here, of not just riding through life in a car at sixty miles per hour but to be vulnerable to all the being, all that surrounds us while we cna be, while we are alive,—this is the essesnce of real mysticism. It is Jesus saying, "the Kingdom/queendom of God is among you." We do not have to seek it afar, it already *is* among us.

This book is about recovering a sense of *simplicity*. What is really necessary for our journeys and what is excess? While I was reading this book the doorbell rang and a streetperson whom I have known for over twenty years was at my door very elated for he had, finally, secured his own living quarters; he could now live in an apartment alone that he could call his own. Somehow there lies a connection between his journey on the streets of Oakland, in and out of jails and back yards, shelters and viaducts, and the pilgrims in this book. Only his journey has been far longer than theirs.

All of life is a pilgrimage and our whole lives long we are learning what is essential and what is less so. That is the lesson we all take to our death beds. Like the pilgrims herein,. this man, who now has AIDS along with his other troubles, was estatic at the news that had befallen him. A home. A goal accomplished. But the journey counted so deeply, the pain and the pleasure of it, the via negativa and the via positiva of it—it was all God-given.

There is so much to learn from the well-chosen and well-spaced reflections by pilgrims offered in these pages. The key is probably to trust one's heart as the reader is invited into the intimacy of other hearts—the wonder of nature, the power of solitude, the strentght of a community of travelers, the awe of the night sky, the invitation a new morning brings, the healing that a good night's sleep, a refreshing meal, a glass of wine, or conversation brings after a long day's journey. This is where a life of simplicity begins: with honoring what is essential and letting go of what is excess. Not only individuals have to learn these truths but communities and nations and even our species has to re-learn these things today.

Much wisdom emerges from the deep and simple observations of the wanderers in this book. One walker confesses: "I feel I have new feet," another that "walking doesn't so much allow me to live in the moment as force me to." Walking is a fine example of what I call "art as meditation." It is a way of calming the reptilian brain and connecting to our deepest self and to God and the universe. This comes through profoundly in the considerations of these wayfarers. Walking takes one into one's soul, as one person tells us, "there's something about the act of walking, its rhythm nudges the memory, brings words, phrases, verses, songs to consciousness." Walking teaches us to slow down. Slow down and take time to experience what is. And what is holy. The result? Often we break into song. And into poetry.

An "enormous silence" brings a "sense of timelessness," testifies another pilgrim. One's "obedience to awareness, my openness to what comes in through all my senses at every moment, moves me toward the *mysterium*," reports another walker.

Mysterium tremendum: the great mystery is the object of all our journeys and knowing this converts all walking to praying.

Choosing to walk a pilgrimage in our day is choosing to leave "couch-potato-itis" behind. It is standing up to the false idols and gods of comfort that so rule over a consumer society. As one wayfarer put it: "One of the things I value about pilgrimage is the psychic violence of an experience that separates us from comfort and familiarity and context, all the habits we didn't know we held so dear." There is a certain fierceness, a kind of warrior energy that emerges, when one chooses to walk for long distances. This is a good thing, for spirituality is not just about bliss but about undergoing whatever it takes to defend what one cherishes. And this takes strength of heart. Yet one does not dwell on the asceticism of it. One dwells on the joy. Joy emerges from these pages and the simple but in many ways radical decisions people made to take the journey. An invitation awaiting us all.

I thank Robert France for gathering these testimonials and for himself undergoing pilgrimage and tasting it deeply and being so in love with this ancient and needed spiritual practice

A book such as this leads us to deep places. As does every pilgrimage. Bring your heart to it. Spirit emerges on every page. Good travels! Bon voyage!

—Matthew Fox
Wisdom University, Oakland

El padre y madre van a rogar y deshazlaguas el niño muer.

Como Santiago pre serot el niño abxera do como se ve.

Sancte Iacobe ora pro nobis.

Introduction

For over one thousand years, the collective imagination (and footsteps!) of millions of people has been captured by the pilgrimage to Santiago de Compostela. At the height of it's popularity in the eleventh and twelfth centuries, hundreds of thousands of individuals from all of Christian Europe are thought to have made the pilgrimage. Though numbers decreased sharply from the seventeenth to the twentieth century, there has recently been a great resurgence with tens of thousands completing the pilgrimage every year. Indeed, the stream of pilgrims sauntering through the fields across France and northern Spain today is such that parts of the route can be almost unbearably crowded in mid-summer. Recently, in recognition that the pilgrimage routes functioned as much as conceptual conduits for establishing Medieval culture as they did physical pathways for wandering travelers, the Way of St. James has been designated a European cultural itinerary.

The physical objective of the pilgrimage was to reach Santiago de Compostela in northwestern Spain, said to be the final resting place of the remains of St. James. Legend has it that St. James traveled to Spain as an evangelist before returning to Jerusalem where he became the first

Apostle to be martyred when he was beheaded by Herod in about 44 A.D. His followers are then said to have placed his body on a ship which, with heavenly help, made landfall on the Galacian coast not far from present-day Santiago de Compostela.

Entombed in a hillside, the body was promptly forgotten. Eight hundred years later, it was "discovered" by a holy hermit aided by visions. Shortly thereafter, St. James ("Sant Iago" in Spanish) was declared the patron saint of Spain, and the devoted began to journey there to pray at his shrine.

The pilgrimage to Compostela increased in popularity after Jerusalem fell to the Moslems at the end of the eleventh century and again one hundred years later. The fact that there is little likelihood that St. James ever set foot in Spain was in no way a deterrent. Nor did the thinly veiled, unsavory aspects associated with the Church's endorsement of the pilgrimage dissuade the faithful.

For the Church, the pilgrimage represented both an opportunity for amassing great wealth and a way to keep the Moslems in southern Spain in check during the Christian Reconquest. In terms of the latter, St. James the Gospel-toting Apostle became transmuted into St. James the sword-yielding Moor slayer.

Even the origin of the pilgrimage's destination name is in question, some believing Compostela to be derived from the Latin *Campus Stellae* or "field of stars," while others—supported by archaeological excavations made in the middle of the twentieth century—think it comes from the Latin word *Compostum*, signifying, much less romantically, "cemetery" at best, or "compost pile" at worst!

But still they came…and came…in the tens of thousands, year after year, throughout the long centuries of strife, disease, and hardship that characterized much of the European Middle Ages.

Medieval pilgrims undertook the journey for a variety of reasons: as a profession of faith, as atonement for realized or imagined sins, as a way to venerate the saints whose relics were contained in many shrines that dotted the route, as a form of prescribed punishment for committed crimes, as a way of obtaining "indulgences" and so reducing time spent in Purgatory, as a means for empowering prayers to alleviate suffering from illness, and finally, simply as a reprieve from the drudgery of life—a grand adventure to see exciting new places and meet interesting new people.

Popes, royalty, nobility, and those who would later be beatified, all undertook the pilgrimage to Santiago de Compostela. The vast majority of pilgrims, however, were simple lay-folk who every spring would rendezvous in a half-dozen meeting places in France and then head off together on foot for the long trip, hoping to return home before the following winter. And, for those that did return, what marvelous stories they could tell of their experiences!

Celebrities upon returning to their native villages, some pilgrims would assume the surnames "King," "Roy," or "Köing" if they had been the fortunate individual in their group who, upon cresting the last hill before the bustling city of Santiago, were the first to have glimpsed the Romanesque towers of the cathedral housing the Apostle's sacred remains. And every successful pilgrim for the rest of his or her days would advertise the pride of their accomplishment by wearing a scallop shell from Finisterre on the Galician coast near Compostela—literally the end of the known Medieval world. Evidence from exhumed graves in northern Europe revealed that some pilgrims would even be buried with their shells—their most cherished possession from the most noted accomplishment or adventure of their lives.

Many pilgrims from the fifteenth century on left accounts of their travels. And in what is regarded as the world's first travel guide—the twelfth century *Codex Calistinus* attributed to the French cleric Amery Picaud—practical notes are provided on travel routes, vernacular architecture, foreign customs, and the like, in a sense, not dissimilar to the many contemporary guidebooks for El Camino de Santiago, as the pilgrimage route has since become known.

Present-day pilgrims undertake the journey for reasons that range from the spiritual to the sportive. For some, the pilgrimage still represents the soulful cleansing sought by their religious Medieval ancestors and possibly reinterpreted through a veneer of modern New Age mysticism; for others, it is a once-in-a-lifetime opportunity to intimately connect with the landscape, architecture, and culture of a foreign location; and for yet others, it represents perhaps nothing more than an athletic challenge, a sort of horizontal Mt. Everest.

Like their Medieval predecessors, contemporary pilgrims often feel motivated to leave behind written records of their journeys for posterity. And yes, though many of these accounts can perhaps embarrassingly veer towards the trite and pedestrian, it is unfair to simply dismiss them altogether as did one historian who labeled them "tediously sentimental and filled with not especially profound spiritual reflections."

How completely different and vastly superior we imagine ourselves to be from our Medieval brethren. And within this comfortable fiction, we time and again parrot the observation that today's pilgrimage is nothing more than a lark or mere holiday compared to that undertaken by those walking the same route five hundred to a thousand years ago.

Certainly there is no doubt that, narrow roads and speed-crazed automobile drivers notwithstanding, the challenges encountered by present-day pilgrims bear no comparison to the dangers faced by Medieval pilgrims from ragging waters, ravenous wolves, and a frightening assortment of cutpurses, brigands, and other nefarious characters. But it would be wrong to suppose that the degree of the physical hardships faced by pilgrims today has in any way lessened through the passage of time. Indeed, the case can be made that the fortitude and endurance required for contemporary pilgrims may actually be greater than that for their predecessors.

With the possible exception of those Medieval pilgrims who had a debilitating disease and were undertaking the journey in hope of a miraculous cure, most pilgrims of yesterday were in far better shape than their modern counterparts. Although not cosmopolitan, the Medieval villager, like Thoreau in nineteenth-century Concord, Massachusetts, would have traveled widely throughout their surrounding countryside, most often by walking. Added to this was the fact that the occupations for many of these individuals would have involved a fair degree of physical exercise on a daily basis.

Lifestyles for many contemporary pilgrims, in contrast, are remarkably more sedentary. It is shocking to realize that by the time many of these pilgrims undertake their seven-hundred to fifteen-hundred-kilometer journey, often upon reaching retirement age, they may not have walked such a distance *cumulatively* in their entire lives, much less doing so on a trek of such a magnitude at a single time! It is no wonder that much prose in modern pilgrim accounts is devoted to recounting the litany of physical ailments brought about by walking. What is truly remarkable is that, despite these burdensome difficulties, so many of these individuals today still somehow find the strength to continue on and complete their journeys.

In Medieval times, pilgrims struggling towards Santiago de Compostela would shout in chorus *"E ultreia! E suseia! Deus aia nos!* (Onward! Upward! God help us!) as encouragement to keep moving ahead when confronted with difficult circumstances. For the reasons explained above, present-day pilgrims facing burdensome fatigue and discomfort obviously require similar motivation to continue their forward progress. And for this I offer the following collection of over two hundred quotations of encouragement compiled from more than thirty contemporary sources.

In his Medieval guide, Amery Picaud divided the Spanish leg of the pilgrimage road into thirteen clearly defined stages corresponding to the following locations: Viscarret, Pamplona, Estella, Najera, Burgos, Fromista, Sahagun, Leon, Rabanal, Villafranca, Triascatela, Palas de Rey, and Santiago. I have adapted this old framework to the thirty-one-day duration that some contemporary guidebooks suggest the journey should take for a fit person.

Within each day, I have arranged the quotations in accordance with the temporal sequence of the old Christian prayer clock—Lauds, Prime, Terce, Sext, None, Vespers, and Compline, which roughly correspond, respectively, to waking up at daybreak (Lauds), early morning just before setting off (Prime), pre-lunch break (Terce), lunch stop (Sext), post-lunch break (None), mid/late afternoon upon arriving at the destination (Vespers), and mid-evening just before going to sleep (Compline). An appropriate quotation can thus be read at each break. In a sense, I have created what might be loosely regarded as a pilgrim's "Book of Hours." Such works were extremely popular devotional texts for the laity in Medieval tumes, providing opportunity for inde-pedent spiritual reflection, and being treasured items to be bequeathed to one's descendants. Using a unique, often personally assembled, Book of Hours, the individ-ual would recite a particular prayer for the hour of the day in relation to the ecclesiastical calendar.

The specific time of day in which a quotation is placed in the album is, as often as not, unrelated to the time of day in which the original pilgrim-scribe first expe-rienced or wrote about the event/feeling. I have attempt-ed to situate the more reflective quotations to be read either early in the morning before heading out the door, or most frequently, in the evening when the day's hard-ships are past and one can finally relax. Many of the quo-tations to be read while enroute during the day are either directly related to beautiful scenery being observed or to encourage one to keep marching forward. For any single quotation source, the overall sequence of quotations scattered throughout the album loosely approximates the linear progression of that pilgrim while enroute. The bulk, but not all, of the quotations are taken from sources describing the pilgrim-scribes' walks through Spain. A smaller fraction arises from accounts describing pilgrimage routes further "upstream" in France, or occasionally from pilgrims who used bicycles for transportation. All share in common a spirit of encouragement, wonder, and joy in their surroundings, in their companions, and in the physicality of the journey itself.

I must end by stating that the quotations assembled here merely scratch the surface of the works from which they were drawn. For every motivational quotation contained herein, many others were left unused due to space constraints. And of course, the overall merits of these source books far transcend the very few words that I have extracted from them here. It is thus my sincere hope that this selection of quotations, in addition to encouraging you to keep placing one foot in front of the other while actually on pilgrimage, will also encourage you to purchase the original sources for armchair reading during your post-pilgrimage recovery back at home, tired feet elevated, glass of French or Spanish wine by your side, wonderful memories in your head, and reflective joy and pride in your heart. And to those individuals about to head out the door to begin your own pilgrimages for the first time, no doubt with a mixture of excitement and trepidation, I can do no better than to wish you: *Ultreia!*

—Robert Lawrence France
Nemo Lodge, Brantwraythwaite, Sheffield

Quotation Album

—A Book of Hours—

STAGE
THE FIRST

Lauds

In the Shadows of Time

That's what I want—to walk with myself and cast a shadow, to walk my way back into my body.

—Kathryn Harrison

Prime

Understanding Freedom's Gift

This was my first day walking the Camino. A shimmer of freedom angled in the shadows before

me. A gift. All I needed, I had in my pack.
Under its weight, I felt my shoulders relax. I
felt relief, though from what I wasn't sure.

—*Mary Victoria Wallis*

Terce

Living a Luminous Dream

The road lies before me: I feel a rush of joy.
For at least three years I've dreamed and imagined this moment and its hard to believe I'm
actually here on the open road, free. My pack
feels lighter, with every third step the rubber tip
of my staff pushes off the ground, my boots
seem to spring up the gradual incline. It's a
luminous day with a high blue sky, billowy
clouds over the crestline above me.

—*Edward F. Stanton*

Sext

On the Delight of Tiredness

After six hours of walking [I was] tired but
overjoyed with the freedom. I felt in the bright
air of the Camino, and delighted too.

—*Mary Victoria Wallis*

None

Pilgrim's Gratitude

As I walked in the very strong sun, I prayed in thanksgiving for this chance to be a pilgrim.

—David Gibson

Vespers

The Way to Experience and Experiencing the Way

This view of the world from the feet is truly unique. The pace at which I move, the time I have to see, the attention of my body to the space in which it breathes—all lead me to believe that this way of experiencing the world has an elemental quality to it; it is somehow basic to any experience—of the world and all I might find there. Being out here is, quite literally, a preparation for experience.

—Lee Hoinacki

Compline

Joyful Cocooning

When I climbed into my sleeping bag at last, my heart was so full of joy and thankfulness I couldn't hold it in.

—Karen Whitehill

STAGE
THE SECOND

Lauds

Walking with a Large Heart

Go lightly, pilgrim, on this earth, / And when you can, alone / In wind and rain find all your mirth, / And in silence make your home.

—*Howard Nelson*

Prime

On Self-Reliance

Somehow there was a feeling of security asso-

ciated with carrying my backpack knowing that I
had everything I needed to survive.

—Sue Kenney

Terce

Out from the Door Where it Began

It was a foggy morning as I set out on a new
adventure.

—David Gibson

Sext

Finding Perfection

Maps are hardly safe indicators of the pictur-
esque, but a small river crossing at the foot of
these woods beckons me on, proving an ideal spot
to lunch and perhaps to paint. It's perfect here.

—Mark Hoare

None

Walking's Result

Walking doesn't so much allow me to live in the
moment as force me to. For the hours each day
when I am on the move, there is no other physi-

cal reality than the combination of the open road,
the weather, and my own body.

—Laurie Dennett

Vespers

Coming to a Realization

I did feel happy! It was unmistakable.

—Mary Victoria Wallis

Compline

Timeless Hunger

*How far backward into my own life would I
have to walk before I might begin to understand
my hunger and what could satisfy it?*

—Kathryn Harrison

Stage The Third

Lauds

Life Cycle of a Pilgrim

Pilgrimage is a penitence and a progress toward death, salvation and a new life.

—*Edward F. Stanton*

The Mysterious Anxiety

We are pilgrims, anxious to make sense of the mystery of why we put ourselves on this road.

—Jack Hitt

Prime

Safe in Spain

Proceeding along, carefree, with no thought of danger at all, I walk...I am in Spain.

—*Lee Hoinacki*

Rituals of Anticipation

We did a lot of fiddling with straps, getting out the camera, peeling off layers under our rain gear, hats on and off. I realized this was going to be a real walk, hard and slow, and that we'd have stinky weather and have to keep going, and I was grinning from ear to ear. I couldn't believe we were actually here and walking.

—*Sophronia Camp*

Terce

Joy and Gratitude

The quietness that surrounded me brought an indescribable sense of peace and joy as I surveyed the cultivated plains that stretched out for miles ahead of me. It was good to be alive in the beauty of the mild morning air and to have the strength and health to be able to walk the pilgrim path.

—*David Gibson*

Paradise Found

I loved the feeling of a portable waterproof house over me. *I* was a pilgrim, going slow, but getting there, a traveling turtle. *We* walked through fields of silent cows, herds of sheep, pigs, and horses. *All* stood as though in a water-soaked trance, not moving, not acknowledging us, somehow in a paradise of safety.

—Shirley MacLaine

Sext

Soaring Sun and Spirits

As the sun rose higher in the sky, we switched to singing, as pilgrims have done for centuries before us.

—Kerry Egan

Like a Corner of Paradise

But flagging spirits were suddenly uplifted as we emerged from the rather gloomy woods and came upon a beautiful mountain meadow carpeted with pink and white daisies....*We* threw ourselves down on the grass to rest weary bones in what seemed like a corner of *Paradise*.

—Emma Poë

None

On the Memory Road

There's something about the act of walking, its rhythm nudges the memory, brings words, phrases, verses, songs to consciousness,

—Edward F. Stanton

Climatic Colours

Bright sun was followed by driving rain. Double rainbows appeared over me, spurring me on. I walked through their colors as they met the ground.

—Shirley MacLaine

Vespers

La Dolce Vita

I...settled down to an enjoyable meal with lots of wine and laugher. The day had covered so much; it seemed like a dream. Light-headed and weary, we winded our way back to the comfort of a night at the Parador.

—Jean Ann Buck

Reflection Through Relaxation

I unpacked my belongings, rolled out my sleeping bag and lay down on it, completely exhausted... With hands clasped behind my head and with a contented grin on my face, I became lost daydreaming about the events that had unfolded that day.

—*Sue Kenney*

Compline

A Well-Earned Rest

Then, after some time—I have no idea how long—my body seems to warm, to become calm... I am quiet.... I sleep.

—*Lee Hoinacki*

The Silence of Deep Time

What there is is enormous silence and solitude. And the result of this was a sense of timelessness, or very slowly moving time; the sensation of a timelessness of progress, that time and distance, the seemingly basic components of all travel, no longer played a leading role in the journey.

—*Conrad Rudolph*

STAGE THE FOURTH

Lauds

The Marvelous Renewal of Sleep

I awaken...and lie here, listening. It's still early, not quite daylight. I try moving my arms and legs a bit in the sleeping bag. No pain. I unzip my bag and get out. Still no pain. I walk to the toilet. I feel fine. Am I the same person I was last night? Am I the same body? I'm actually ready to start walking again, eager in fact.

—Lee Hoinacki

Walking Deep into Oneself

By living the simple life of a pilgrim, everyday just walking, eating, drinking, contemplating and sleeping—I would embark on a new life journey. This gave me the opportunity to finally be alone to walk into the shadows of the darkness and the healing light of my own true self.

—Sue Kenney

Walking as Prayer

Just like walking, prayer is the state of being off-balance—of moving, of not being able to stay in one place even if you want to because some force of nature won't allow it.

—Kerry Egan

Prime

The Benefits of an Obedience to Awareness

Every morning, I go farther into a strange world of surprises, walking into a new place on a soil never before touched by me, meeting people whose existence I had only imagined. My obedience to awareness, my openness to what comes in through all my senses at every moment, moves me

toward the mysterium that lies at the end of this
journey. How fantastic the rewards of attention.

—*Lee Hoinacki*

Delirium

Our little friends the larks were singing above
our heads. A truly perfect morning. I felt quite
delirious with the beauty and joy of being alive
and of being able to make this amazing journey.

—*Emma Poë*

Means and Ends

It felt good to walk, good to have a purpose and
a destination.

—*Kerry Egan*

Terce

Understanding the Happiness of Purpose

What was going through my mind was the realization of how happy I was, unencumbered with
anything more than I needed, my energies direct-
ed solely to the accomplishment of today's purpose.

—*Laurie Dennett*

Circumventing a Life of Regret

I am being introduced to experiences whose existence I never expected, which I could never have dreamed of. To imagine...I might have died without knowing this.

—Lee Hoinacki

Surfacing Through Silence

Walking, I soon discovered, creates a pool of deep silence in which all personal issues can float to the surface and become accessible to deeper scrutiny.

—David Gibson

Sext

Landscape Longing

I found myself in a countryside so beautiful that there was a palpable sense of enchantment, a place far from anywhere, a land that seemed to have been wholly untouched by time.

—Conrad Rudolph

Working Limbs

My feet and legs were holding up just fine.

—Bob Tuggle

The Camino as Cloister

As I walked, my mind eased into a calm, meditative state.

—Sue Kenney

None

The Presumed Eternity of Stone

We modern pilgrims...plod our way along the road of St. James, but our names are written in water, whereas those anonymous masons and stone-cutters of eight hundred years ago, when they tarried in this narrow street where I linger today, left as a token of their passing some tiny individualized figure or ornament, which, in a flash, illustrates the universal significance of the pilgrimage.

—Walter Starkie

A Memory of the Moment

I was strangely aware as though time had divided and I was looking back at the moment along a corridor of years, that this is one of the sights of my life to which my thoughts would turn.

—Laurie Dennett

Becoming Landscape

It was more as if the landscape very slowly passed us by than we it. Sometimes, it seemed as if we became part of the landscape.

—Conrad Rudolph

Vespers

Smelling the Flowers

Despite the mud and overcast sky, it was a wonderful journey today, with plenty of birdsong, banks of golden cowslips...violets, wild columbine, orchids...oregano, majoram, lots of gorse...vetch and a beautiful blue flower I didn't know.

—Jean Ann Buck

Weighing the Benefits

The weather alternated between sun and rain, but for the most part it was an enjoyable day of walking....It was challenging, but interesting and fun.

—Bob Tuggle

Peace and Tranquility

There had been moments during the day when I felt lost and certainly very tired; now as I lay down, completely rested, I was filled with a sense of peace and tranquility.

—David Gibson

Compline

Experiential Richness of the Road

One week on the Camino has contained more experience, more change than a year of my normal life, maybe several years; one day can hold a little birth, death and rebirth; one hour, one minute, seconds may offer an abyss or a joy like the one I feel now, free, without the watch, moving with my staff at my own speed, absorbing the landscape, always looking ahead on the road where each curve hides a promise.

—Edward F. Stanton

The World at its Best

I felt strong and confident...All was well with the world, and in the sunset outside the window it looked the best possible of all worlds.

—Nicholas Luard

Anticipation of Adventure

I was looking forward to the adventures of the next day. What has amazed me so far in the camino was that on no occasion yet had I felt any disinclination to face another day. Despite the moments when I had been very tired at the end of the a day's walking, I had always risen the following day refreshed and ready to embark on a new adventure.

—David Gibson

STAGE
THE FIFTH

Lauds

Deep Time

Among the promises of Santiago is an altered relationship with time, the attempt to measure it step by step. Not to defeat time, nor to fight against its relentlessness, but to perceive time, one of the faces of God—a face routinely obscured by our modern multitasking lives.

—Kathryn Harrison

Born Again

I get up early, find that I am marvelously renewed—a new man!—eager to be out on the camino as soon as possible.

—Lee Hoinacki

Scallops as Clams

I was happy as a clam, if sleepless. What I realized in the wee hours was that the affability and excitement was due to the fact that everyone had chosen to be here and was pumped up for the route. In that respect it was like being at Disneyland, where families look a lot better than they do in supermarket isles conducting their day-to-day business. Everyone here was flashing guidebooks, comparing notes, cooking, hogging the radiators to dry out clothing, sharing stories.

—Sophronia Camp

The Core of a Pilgrimage

Pilgrimage's emotional center is hope.

—Kerry Egan

Prime

Feet First

I feel as if I have new feet.

—Lee Hoinacki

Praise for Companionship

The sun was beginning to make its appearance in the morning sky. There was little conversation between us; yet we felt comfortable simply being together along the route.

—David Gibson

Mesmerized by Light

From a glassless window high on one wall a beam of sunlight traverses the room, specks of dust dancing in its, making a little square of light on the floor....I don't know how long I stand still, forgetting myself, immersed in this moment now, here, always, at peace with myself and the world.

—Edward F. Stanton

Following the Body's Lead

It was me who had to learn what simplicity is and what work (walk) really means. I realized the importance of the rhythm of life and of one's body which must be followed.

—Judy Foot

Terce

Ghosts

I can almost hear the muffled tread of feet along the road.

—Laurie Dennett

Smiling Steps

I walked with my shoulders pulled back, standing tall, smiling inwardly as I discovered this joyful expression within my being.

—Sue Kenney

The Privilege of Walking

Gradually my body would find a more flowing way to move. My feet didn't stop hurting, but I tasted the morning's fresh air and the huge privilege of another day of walking. Looking forward to the day's scents and sounds, and feeling the pleasure of my hips and thigh muscles in a smooth flowing walk made the hurt seem smaller. Little by little my stride lengthened.

—*Maria & Donald Schell*

Forgetting About Blisters

Once I was on the way again the blisters throbbed for a few moments and then gave up the attempt to add to the difficulties. Half an hour later the problems of the day might never have existed. I was swinging along as if now acclimatized to the heat and enjoying the route.

—*Bert Slader*

Sext

Following Others' Footsteps

We followed a tree-lined pathway where the ancient pilgrim's way was worn into the stones. The sun shone on the matted surface of the rock, highlighting the gouges and the grooves. Lost in daydreaming, I could almost see the pilgrim's footsteps in the stones.

—*Karen Whitehill*

Creating an Autobiography by Walking

When walking becomes what you do, all that you do, when that meditation becomes a natural part of the rhythm of your day, you become very good at listening....After awhile, you begin to realize that not all thoughts necessarily sound like your own, that there are subtle, fleeting emotions that usually get overlooked, and longings and desires you didn't know you had. You begin to see that many events in your life are not as random as they first appear. You begin to suspect and then to be sure, when you listen intently for so long, that something you did not notice before exists in you, within your mind, in your heart.

—*Kerry Egan*

Halcyon Days Ahead

The day turned out to be one of the finest, most golden days I've ever spent—a time to hold in the mind, to remember and cherish in the darkest of icy mid-winters to come. We climbed through the mist, broke out of it, and suddenly we were in sunlight. Shining, glowing, luminous sunlight folded round our shoulders on a scented southern wind.

—*Nicholas Luard*

Orpheus Ascending

As Orpheus, I travel / Through caverns of the heart / To recover, like Eurydice, My innocence, my trust.

—Howard Nelson

None

Reaching Across Time

About halfway up, I had the distinct impression that it was St. James himself who was pushing me on from behind. It was a blinding revelation, or anything that seemed particularly out of the ordinary at that stage, just the sense of a kindly, practical, no-nonsense sort of character lending a helping hand; a feeling that grew on me gradually. Several times I was almost on the point of turning around to thank him, and it was only later that I thought of this as odd, for I did not for a moment believe that St. James had ever set foot in Spain, dead or alive.

—Bettina Selby

Bidding Civilization Adieu

The paint marks took us off the main road almost immediately, and the beauty of the fields

and hillsides filled out hearts with happiness.
We sang songs.

—*Karen Whitehill*

The Crystallization of Time

We seemed to be on a glass mountain. At first
we actually thought, with disgust, that the
remains of broken bottles littered the path. Then,
when we looked closer, we found that many of the
stones beneath our feet were crystals which glint-
ed in the sun.... The momentary glister must have
cheered many weary pilgrims as they toiled over
this obstacle down the centuries. As we left one
plain behind, walked briefly across a level
plateau...and were then greeted by another sweep
of open yellow landscape reaching to the far horizon, I felt as close to all those who had gone
before us as at any moment on our pilgrimage.

—*Robin Hanbury-Tenison*

Appreciating the Individuality
and Poetics of Place

There is something solid about where I am—at
every moment. And all my senses seem to be
more open, more aware; they seem to be taking in
much more. It's as if I'm plowing through infi-
nitely different perceptions, for with every step I

am in a different place, and each place has its own unique character. At each step if I stop and sense where I am, what is around me, I know, I see, that it is different from the previous place. Is this what poets mean when they celebrate the wonders of creation?

—Lee Hoinacki

Vespers

The Solace of Rest

I leaned back against the tough, crimped bark of the oak tree, with its many branches and its little leaves spread like a green-speckled quilt above me. An emptiness enveloped me like air wafting around a clothesline without its sheets. I had the sensation of being completely without fear.

—Mary Victoria Wallis

Painful Loss

After the difficulty of the day I was amazed to find that all the pain was easily assuaged by a hot bath, the companionability of strangers, and a drink.

—Sophronia Camp

The Paradox of Being Anchored in Movement

I'm also aware of the contact between this world, no longer completely mine, and my new life on the Camino alone, walking on aching feet but free, doing what I only dreamed of doing once, in touch with my own steps, close to the road, the land, the weather.

—Edward F. Stanton

Solace of Feet and Soul

As I took my boots off in my room...I had seldom felt happier. In spite of the snow and the rain, the journey so far had been wonderful, a physically taxing but joyous tramp through some of the loveliest landscapes in Europe.

—Nicholas Luard

Compline

Healing Sleep

My mind floated into a deep healing sleep in anticipation of the next day. I was excited and nervous at the same time wondering what was in store for me.

—Sue Kenney

The Importance of Novelty over Comfort

I remind myself that one of the things I value about pilgrimage is the psychic violence of an experience that separates us from comfort and familiarity and context, all the habits we didn't know we held so dear.

—Kathryn Harrison

Lifting the Cloud of Unknowing

Perhaps it is that the Camino makes it easier to sense a God who is always there but is easy to ignore. A God one has to have courage to fall into, whether through walking or love or grief or, through the final prayer of this pilgrimage, remembering.

—Kerry Egan

Gratitude for the Support of Other Pilgrims

In spite of the exhaustion and pain, I am here, I've completed another stage in this journey, supported during the day, by those who preceded me, comforted, at night, by the friendliness and companionship of those resting with me here. A great peacefulness envelopes me. I am walking into a new world, a new place...that I did not know existed.

—Lee Hoinacki

STAGE
THE SIXTH

Lauds

Time Travel

The road is a shared experience in two senses. Like any journey it involves movement forward through space, but it also involves a kind of time-travelling into the past. In discovering the road for yourself, you share the experience of thousands of people over the course of a millennium.

—Laurie Dennett

On the Difference Between
Pilgrims and Tourists

A pilgrim is not a tourist. You have a deeper experience preciously because you are not an observer in the traditional sense of the word....You are part of the cultural landscape, part of the original reason for being and the history of many of the towns through which you pass....Yours is the experience of fully reconciled alienation: the pilgrim at once the complete insider, the total outsider. This is why the pilgrimage is not a tour, not a vacation, not at all a trip from point A to point B, but a journey that is both an experience and a metaphor rather than an event.

—*Conrad Rudolph*

Regeneration and Renewal

Anyone's journey to Santiago must contain many small deaths and rebirths.

—*Edward F. Stanton*

Prime

Feet, Don't Fail Me Now

We were up at daybreak and off by seven-fifteen. My feet felt much, much better.

—*Sophronia Camp*

A Day Off in Paradise

We couldn't have chosen a better place to take a day off. The sun shone, the birds sang, the river splashed across the stones, the breeze whispered in the trees. The twentieth century seemed a forgotten nightmare.

—Ben Nimmo

Security in Progress

There was a sense of security in putting one foot in front of the other for the sheer reason I was moving forward.

—Sue Kenney

Terce

Into Big-Sky Country

I felt strong and fit. I strode out...across the rising planes of moorland. There was nothing except the harsh cold wind in my face, a few ruined walls, the still bare yellow grass with the snow-melt only just gone from the high pastures, the occasional cluster of leafless beech trees, and a sky, a sky that reached for ever. I had never seen anything like that sky....I had seldom felt such a sense of freedom, of exhilaration. I went on faster and faster.

—*Nicholas Luard*

Entering a Varied Landscape

When J start out again, the rain slackens and then stops. A lovely, fresh spring day lights my path, and everything appears especially pleasant. J pass through fields, an occasional small village, climb into mountainous hill country, and walk through a stout and healthy-looking forest. Already an incredible variety of scenery and settings, yet the day is still young.

—*Lee Hoinacki*

Buenas Dias

This was already becoming one of my favorite days.

—*Tim Moore*

Sext

Capturing the Magic

The ice on the puddles is thick, riddled with strange latticework and cloudy contour lines. J contemplate painting: perhaps a detail of a puddle or the way the ice follows the imprint of a tractor tyre, like water in the fingers of a fjord. But fleeting shimmering magic such as this is surely the realm of the photographer — or perhaps it's never to be satisfactorily recorded, but only really felt at first hand and deeply breathed in.

—Mark Hoare

Lost and Found

We stopped and checked the map, which indicated that we should cross a paved road soon. We held our breath until we came to the paved road, Shortly thereafter, we found the trail markers.

—Jim & Eleanor Clem

How Green Were the Valleys

It was difficult work, but the scenery was beautiful. We could see small streams and green valleys below as we trudged up the path which was dark and eerie due to the large overhanging branches of the trees.

—Bob Tuggle

None

Explaining a Minor Miracle

As the sun mounts higher I sweat more—a

clean sweat in the dry air, without the acrid smell you notice when you perspire in the city. You may not believe this but its true, another daily miracle on the Road to Santiago.

—Edward F. Stanton

Taking Time to Smell the Coffee

We were not in any hurry, and wanted to enjoy the adventures in full measure. Thus we took to stop where we wanted, and had plenty of chocolate and coffee-stops during the day.

—Knud Helge Robberstad

Joyful Toe Liberation

At the top of the village, a path led to a large field surrounded by tumbledown walls. I climbed through a gap and found a shady spot under trees to while away the hours until everyone arrived. I took off my rucksack, spread my fleece on the ground and threw off my socks and boots. It was wonderful just sitting there in the peace and quiet. My feet cooled off. I felt quite elated to be alone and resting in this beautiful spot.

—Jean Ann Buck

Vespers

Auditory Solipsism

In the late afternoon, when we were tired and trudging along silently, I became aware of sound. The birds had quieted down, and all I heard was Us—our sticks clicking along, water jostling with every step, a regular swish of nylon pack against a sweaty back, and various rhythmic squeaks of plastic clasps; and our crunching footsteps—a sort of mini-world of noise, where every sound was attached in some way to our own movement.

—*Sophronia Camp*

Savoring Steps

As we were walking on the trail today, everything felt great. No aches or pains. I consciously made myself enjoy every step.

—*Jim & Eleanor Clem*

The Art of Walking

The art of walking every day had the pleasing effect of clearing my mind and awakening my body in a familiar rhythm I had come to love. The passing scenery was experienced in a height-

ened state of awareness, with all my senses
engaged; my eyes captured the pictures, my nose
breathed in the aroma of the village, my ears listened to the music of the language, my mouth
savored the full-flavored camino air, while my
feet touched the earth walked by millions of pilgrims before me.

—Sue Kenney

Compline

Thoughts While Supine

It's taken me more than a third of the way to
Compostela to break out of my solitude....Each
traveller must follow his own rhythm on the road,
Mine tells me that a change is growing in me as
surely as I can feel my skin, warmed by the sun
and wine, against the cool sheets of this bed.
Let the new moon be the start of a new cycle for
me too, in my body and heart.

—Edward F. Stanton

Benefits of Bivouacking

The sun was setting, suffusing the fields with
soft, pastel light. We found a place to camp in a
grove of poplars just off of the trail. No longer
worried about sleeping outdoors, I actually

looked forward to it—a welcome change from stuffy rooms. We spread out our sleeping bags and sat down on them; watching the peach-colored sun set into the golden hills, watching the star-filled Milky Way come out in the night sky. The air smelled like fresh-cut grass. As we drank some cognac...we listened to the buzzing cicadas, the breeze ruffling the trees, and the distant clanging of church bells.

—Ellen O. Feinberg

The Road Within

Over time, the road takes up residence within us and becomes a way to something else.

—Jack Hitt

**STAGE
THE SEVENTH**

Lauds

Finding Self

In solitude, the pilgrim faces into the inner journey of self-knowledge alone; each person finds themselves longing for these moments along the camino.

—David Gibson

Happy Days Are Here Again

I count the days that followed as among the happiest of my life, days of ease, well-being, contentment.

—Nicholas Luard

Prime

The Joy of Walking

It felt so good to be walking again that I found myself consciously putting on the brakes to keep from running. The pack fits me so perfectly that I long ago ceased to be very aware of it. In the excitement of reaching the halfway mark, I strode along singing at the top of my lungs.

—*Laurie Dennett*

Bidding Blisters 'Bye

Instead of agony, walking was almost a pleasure. My blisters had healed and I was used to the weight of my pack. I felt good.

—*Ellen O. Feinberg*

Terce

Walking with Simplicity

Another beautiful walking day....We climbed up and up out of the valley, stopping to look back again and again. We continued down into the next valley to more of the same. I felt very strong and energized today for the first time, as if I was simply walking—not hiking or climbing or pushing or struggling.

—*Sophronia Camp*

Existential Acceptance

For the fist time, I realized time was passing. Life had become a scatter of images as brilliant as stained-glass shards. I'd lost track of the days, the weeks, everything but the now, bright and compelling.

—*Ben Nimmo*

Sext

The Wet Savior

On reaching the countryside I heard a distant rumble....Slowly they approached and the first of at least one hundred tractors and trailers passed by, some occasionally turning along tracks to the right or left. I realized how incredibly fortunate I had been. Had it not poured with rain in the middle of the night, I would by now have been coated with dust and coughed and sneezed all day. As it happened, the rain dampened the soil and I was saved.

—*Christabel Watson*

The Solidarity of Pilgrims

From walking alone, I had come across others, even without seeing them, I knew that I was part of something bigger. Was this strange feeling a solidarity with unknown pilgrims the sensation which motivated the medieval traveller?

—Andrea Kirby

None

A Transcendental World

When the climbing ends, I feel that I'm in a new place, as if I'm walking on top of the world, as if I'm in a place altogether above the normal world, the everyday world.

—Lee Hoinacki

From Saunter to Gallop

It was a glorious sun-filled day, the...countryside was green, glowing, rich with scented grass in its summer pastures; I felt fit and buoyant. I strode out so strongly that, by early afternoon, I'd caught up with the others.

—Nicholas Luard

Vespers

Placing Suffering in Context

To see the greatest mystery of their faith re-enacted amid such surroundings must have made the sufferings of the road appear mere trifles.

—*Laurie Dennett*

Developing an Intimate Awareness

On the camino, I've come to an intimate aware-ness of the earth, the air, and water. The soil powerfully presses itself into me with every step; the air fuels my lungs with fresh life in every breath; the pure, sparkling water of the springs continually revives my spirit.

—*Lee Hoinacki*

Compline

Temptation of Silence

I succumb to the temptation of silence, not talk-ing to a soul all day or night, sleeping alone in a field.

—*Edward F. Stanton*

Thanksgiving and Belonging

The feeling on the Camino had changed...from a feeling of distressed introspection, of fear of what was lurking in my own mind to betray me, to the warm feeling of Thanksgiving night, once dessert is over and everyone is playing board games, a strength and comfort in the people around you, a feeling of not being alone.

—*Kerry Egan*

Stage
The Eighth

Lauds

Carpe Diem

Every day is an adventure, potentially surreal, and where feelings so unconnected with modern existence become a part of everyday life.

—Conrad Rudolph

A Good Kind of Drunk

Drunk on stars, I've hardly slept. Yet I don't feel tired. Watching the sky has calmed my mind and given me a cold new kind of energy.

—Edward F. Stanton

Prime

Solar Expectations and Appreciations

I had grown accustomed to anticipating the beauty and peace I experienced just before the sun found its way over the horizon.

—Sue Kenney

Strategy for Hitting the Trail Running

Stoked by a...breakfast spectacular I hit the road with sturdy enthusiasm.

—Tim Moore

Terce

Miracle of Healing

At my breakfast stop at 11am I pulled off my splint....I never even felt my leg, and the splint disappeared to the bottom of my rucksack. How could it have healed so quickly? Perhaps the answer was another miracle.

—Christabel Watson

Appreciating Creation

I walked slowly. The only sound was the wind

whispering to itself. Tiny birds perched sound-
lessly on the twigs of shrubs standing paralyzed
by the road. A cricket rubbed its wings. It was
so dry my nose felt light inside and nothing
pressed my skin. But the scene was dreamingly
fluid like a transparent lake, a swirl of warmth
and yellow grass, islands of shrubs trembling
like water in the heat, rounded mountains vapor-
izing into the sky.

—Mary Victoria Wallis

Sext

The Distraction of Scenery

It was easy for me to keep my mind off my
pumping legs and tired shoulders, with so much
scenery to look at.

—Karen Whitehill

Treasuring Mystical Landscapes

I looked around as I walked. The hillsides
were mystical, possessing treasures of experience that were there for us to hear if we would
open up to them.

—Shirley MacLaine

None

Shortening Shadows

A long quiet walk over the meseta; / Frost crisp underfoot; the sky an unbroken blue; / Larksong; watching my shadow slowly shorten / And edge towards the north; feeling my shoulders / Warm to the sun, and hearing that first cicada.

—*Neil Curry*

Making an Impression

There were masses of cornflowers and daises growing profusely among the scarlet poppies. An impressionist painting come to life.

—*Jean Ann Buck*

Vespers

Following the Advice of Napoleon's Cook

Then dinner came. It was one of the best, the richest, the most handsome and resplendent meals I have ever eaten.

—*Nicholas Luard*

A Grand Buccal Union

It felt as though my body had turned to laughter, and for just a moment I felt a burning and surging love for all those people surrounding me. I wanted to kiss each one.

—*Kerry Egan*

Compline

Heaven on Earth

When the moon sets, we see the Milky Way as men and women saw it in the great days of pilgrimage, To my wonder it's not a uniform stripe across the heavens but an organic thing with arms, branches, tributaries, inlets, lakes, peninsulas—luminous, complex, alive. El Camino de las Esrellas, the Road of Stars.

—*Edward F. Stanton*

Self-Discovery

Over the past few weeks I have become aware of reserves of physical strength I never knew I possessed.

—*Laurie Dennett*

STAGE
THE NINTH

Lauds

Mind-Body Melding

In the beginning I had thought it strange that
pilgrimage, which was supposed to focus on the
spirit, made me so very conscious of the weak-
ness of my flesh. Once that had seemed like a
contradiction. Now I realized that the physical
suffering was a way to experience the spirit: the
two were complimentary.

—Ellen O. Feinberg

Across the Time-Space Continuum

One...was not only walking across space, but across time as well.

—Kerry Egan

Confraternity

There are no real strangers on the camino. All are united in the common purpose, and even passing and saluting without talking to them creates a sense of oneness with the wider world of pilgrimage.

—David Gibson

Prime

Tips for Practicing the Rhythm Method

I found I was walking more on the balls of my feet because I felt lighter. The thistles cut my thighs and my legs, but it didn't hurt. I got into a kind of spiritual march where the rhythm of my steps echoed my breathing. My shoes hit the dirt and my arms swung in rhythm with the thumping of my backpack. I swung my arms over my head so that my hands wouldn't cramp. When I stopped, I listened to the sounds of nature.

—Shirley MacLaine

Landscape Appreciation

How good it was to be alive. The pain in my feet had eased considerably, and this allowed me to concentrate on the beauty of the surrounding countryside.

—David Gibson

Daydreams and Silent Words

We were off again at dawn. It was a quiet and gentle day along sun-filled tracks and lanes. A day for thoughts and occasional speculative talk. We unlaced our boots and ate our midday meal piece in a glade starred with late summer flowers and surrounded by thickets of gorse. We passed through a couple of silent hamlets without even a barking dog to harass us....We walked on.

—Nicholas Luard

Terce

Becoming the Camino

Hours of constant rain acted like a mantra arousing my senses and elevating the level of conscious awareness I was experiencing. Soon my skin began to take on the aroma of nature, absorbing the fresh scent of the rain soaked forest. I was becoming the Camino.

—Sue Kenney

Hydrophilia Satisfied

We crossed the road at one point and spied a new fountain pouring into a waist-high rectangular pool. I couldn't resist a foot soak in spite of the early hour and no real need; it was an irresistibly inviting pool made out of a warm, golden stone.

—Sophronia Camp

A Feeling of Simply Joy

Each time...I eventually come to an arrow again. Somehow, my sense of direction—or my guardian angel—saves me. A feeling of simple joy...a great sigh of happy relief when the arrow appears again.

—Lee Hoinacki

Sext

Road to Happiness

Feelings of well-being swept over me as I walked along the camino.

—David Gibson

Self-Appreciation

I was conscious of enjoying my own company despite all the enjoyment I've had of late in other people's.

—Laurie Dennett

Entering a Living Painting

Each of us, wordlessly drawn to the scene, stopped one by one at a little distance from each other, to gawk. We stood in silence for some minutes, taking in the brilliant colors of the fields, earth, sky, and the sounds of the sheep bells and the shepherd and his wife calling and whistling, and the movement of the dogs, sheep, and shepherds across the fields—another moment spent in a living painting, incredibly beautiful, and somehow holy.

—Sophronia Camp

None

Glimpsing the Edge

Seeing the horizon at all times, I come to know what it is to live with a horizon—an experience lost to most modern people.

—Lee Hoinacki

Holy Water

There I lay against the side of the trough allowing the spray from the gushing fountain to sprinkle my hair and sweatshirt. And bathing my feet in the cool water was simply heavenly.

—*David Gibson*

Without Words

We tracked upward and then downwards, speaking little, There was no need to talk. It was a time of contentment, a time for reflection.

—*Nicholas Luard*

Vespers

Learning the Wisdom of Walking

I also realized that all my life I had been seeking, seeking activities, seeking meanings and reasons for what I was doing and seeking deep and meaningful relationships. I clearly knew that I had found a great deal whilst walking.

—*Judy Foot*

Fairies Wearing Boots

I walked through oak groves, pine woods, and a eucalyptus forest, imagining myself a princess in an ancient fairyland. Even though these paths were near to modern towns I could not see or hear the towns as I walked through the woods that seemed to belong to another time. I was alone with my thoughts but felt the company of others who had walked the road for centuries before me.

—Linda L. Lasswell

The Luxury of Physical Exercise

For the first time since I started I felt under no pressure to finish the day quickly, no desperation to cover the distance, but I felt only the luxury of physical exercise, the muscles starting to warm and wake, and the sun and wind on my face.

—Andrea Kirby

Compline

Blessings Big and Small

Well we were both still alive, I hadn't seen a cockroach or had a single stone in my boot.

—Tim Moore

The Illuminated Path

My eyes adjusted to the darkness as it descended upon us. Without the distraction of street-lights the natural glow of the moon lit our way. Like a gift from heaven, there were tiny white stones all along the path up the mountainside. The moonlight touched the surface of these stones reflecting just enough light onto the path to be able to see the way.

—Sue Kenney

A Growing Peace and the Measure of Hope

Now we know the change must begin inside ourselves because the Camino has calmed the war in our own hearts. We saw the haste, the greed and solitude in ourselves and others; on the Road we've exchanged them for a growing peace, unselfishness and solidarity between pilgrims. Walking, eating, sleeping, suffering side by side we've forgotten the boundaries between ourselves and between sexes, countries, classes, ages. This is part of what we were seeking, the measure of our hopes.

—Edward F. Stanton

STAGE
THE TENTH

Lauds

Through the Wormhole

All I want is what my feet deliver: simultaneous communion with those dead and those yet to be, walking myself, step by step, lower lower, into a deeper consciousness of mortality, each life unbearably small, impossibly brief, while time and history flood ever backward and forward.

—*Kathryn Harrison*

Establishing Clear Choices

Walking the pilgrim route helps clarify our pri-orities.

—David Gibson

Prime

Mind over Matter

My feet are better after a day's rest....To hell with blisters!

—Edward F. Stanton

Olfaction and Adaptation

The colours and hues were striking and we mar-velled at the view around us as we drank in the smell of gorse and broom and brushed through the tall heather. My feet were much better as my new canvas and leather boots were stretching and adapting to the shape of my feet.

—Jean Ann Buck

Terce

Welcoming the Clean Slate of a New Day

Deep vales cut into rounded hills. A mountain like a lumpy hand. Cool wind. The dull orange scars of landslide or soil erosion. A village seen far off at the bottom of a torrent. Choughs barking in the wind above. Slate to walk on, crunching underfoot, soft and slimy looking like wet coal. Squeezing between two soft bushes of furse, feeling its caress. The wind on my face wakes me, it is the embrace of a new day, the sun shining at last, coming down from the wildness. In the far distance there are smoking chimneys, industry; here, only the air and the cry of birds.

—*Andrea Kirby*

The Secret to Forward Momentum

I walked the Camino now with a calmness, and I walked faster because of it.

—*Shirley MacLaine*

Sext

Timeless Benediction

There's nothing quite like receiving a blessing to renew energy and resolve. I think I crossed over, in that moment of blessing, from interpreting my pilgrimage as private undertaking to understanding that I was a drop in an almost timeless flow.

—*Sophronia Camp*

Entering a Dreamscape

It was a quiet and golden descent. The air was still and sweet. We were thronged all about with the murmured sounds and rich scents of an ancient landscape. Waters tumbled over rocks in the valley's river beside us. Halfway down we came on a deserted farmhouse, nestling in the woods like an abandoned bird's nest....The valley was a place of dreams.

—Nicholas Luard

None

The Happiness of Silence

When we stopped for lunch, sitting amongst the heather, a great peace and tranquility descended. I felt an inner sense of real happiness, a perfect silence that was unbroken by the wondrous clouds busily passing across the sky, clouds that I had only ever seen before in the frescos on church walls.

—Judy Foot

Lessons from the Sixties

We had a good rhythm going, so we decided to keep truckin'. Up, up, and up.

—Jim & Eleanor Clem

Vespers

Recognizing the Road of Life

The routine of a day's walking and a night's rest in a simple refuge had become my life. It felt comfortable and normal. I felt that I had become part of the Camino.

—Judy Foot

Cleaning the Belfry

The Camino de Santiago has allowed me to get away from it all...to clean the cobwebs from my mind and come to terms with my life, to search for a new peace inside myself.

—Edward F. Stanton

Compline

Warming to Climate's Effects

One advantage of this cold weather was the marvelous light and cloud effects, and nowhere were these more magnificent than the evening I spent in this pilgrim village. The mackerel clouds had darkened a shade to absolute perfection, and the grey church and houses against the darkly luminous sky seemed tremendously beautiful and tragic at the same time, reflecting as they did what was temporal and passing against what was eternal. 'The sad hour of Compline' was the phrase that came to mind again as I composed my photographs.

—Bettina Selby

Holistic Awareness

I was feeling a whole person, at last I knew exactly who I was but I also knew that when I did return home I would be a different person to the one who had left. Not dramatically different, but with a much greater awareness of myself.

—Judy Foot

STAGE THE ELEVENTH

Lauds

Pride in Achieving Rather Than in Achievement

Now, when it is almost on the horizon, I realized that, while I rejoiced in the achievement, I rejoiced even more in the achieving.

—Laurie Dennett

Similar to Shackleton

We had walked through the pain, the exhaustion. We still ached, we still got tired, but we had endured. And more than endured: we had overcome our limits and changed them in the process.

—Ellen O. Feinberg

Prime

Music of the Ages

I sat down with my back against a tree and closed my eyes to listen. It was as if I was hearing these sounds for the first time. The effect was like meditation music and all the tension of rushing through life had now disappeared. I opened my eyes and saw a dream landscape. Between the trees was a prospect of miles of countryside streaked with eddies of early morning mist and ridge behind low ridge as far as the eyes could see.

—Bert Slader

Interplanetary Travel

The countryside ahead of me is totally flat that I can see the curve of the earth at the horizon. As the sun slowly rises, the reddish hue of the sky blends into the red clay of the road and fields, and I imagine myself on another planet, not just in another land.

—Karen Whitehill

Terce

Overcoming Camino Mythconceptions

It was a steady uphill, but not nearly as bad as we had expected. The way people talked about this section of the Camino had us thinking that we were in for a very steep, difficult climb.

—Jim & Eleanor Clem

Trust and Uncertainty

Exhausted or exultant, there is no avoiding / The ghosts of those who plodded along this road....There are destinations which demand / That we ourselves have been the journey, / And it is some way yet to Santiago. / Maybe I've brought too much; guide books and maps / Can blur the edge of our uncertainties. / Travelling on with a trust in what was there, / They walked their faith. I walk their elegy.

—Neil Curry

Sext

A Loved and Layered Landscape

Despite the weather, when I raised my head I was struck by the gentle beauty of the landscape.

There was a quality of harmony about it, the sense of a land long tamed, but treated lovingly by its inhabitants.

—Laurie Dennett

Savoring Eye Candy

Sitting on an old fallen tree, we stopped to allow our eyes to feast on the surrounding scene. The meandering stream as it wound its way through the valley created a picture of Spain at its best. No words of mine could describe the peace and contentment that filled my being at that moment. It was sheer bliss.

—David Gibson

None

Slowing Down to Smell the Manure

Once...it would have bothered me to stop, to lose time on the road. Now, I enjoy the pause, taking in the sight, smelling the comfortable odors of manure and smoke coming from nearby.

—Edward F. Stanton

Confidence in Progress

The walking was on good turf now, crackly or

crunchy with stones and gravel, and on roads; no more mud, no more slipping, but back to the pleasure of a confidently placed foot on the ground, and the crisp sound of progress at each step.

—Andrea Kirby

Vespers

Resplendent in Wonder

As I got closer to Compostela, each day seems more lovely, more filled with charm, more resplendent with wonders.

—Lee Hoinacki

The Camino as Midwife

This I have learned from the Camino...the body can be surpassed, shed like a snake's molting skin. My old body has died; in many ways I have also died to my old self.

—Edward F. Stanton

Compline

Uisce Baetha

The landscape stretched below me in gradual,

grassy slopes. The farmer's fields were blurred by the distance and the evening haze. The air cooled as the sun dropped to the horizon. Soon I was mesmerized by an outstanding crimson and golden sunset. As I ate the last of the cheese and bread the sky grew darker. I wrapped myself in my sleeping bag to ward off the creeping chill. I remembered the flask with the Glemorangie scotch. I found it in my bag, took a few sips, and relaxed into the evening.

—Linda L. Lasswell

Raise High the Roofbeams, Pilgrims

A wonderfully symbolic idea: the pilgrims building the basilica as they walked, the very act of pilgrimage creating the church in which they would worship; both pilgrimage and building being acts of worship as valid in their way as the sacrament of the Mass, and as heartfelt. Every footstep another stone in the wall of the church.

—Andrea Kirby

STAGE
THE TWELFTH

Lauds

Timeless Lure of Sacred Geography

Whatever we imagine, there is something on the road beneath the star-filled skies, in the shrine of Compostela or beyond by the sea—a memory, a presence, an intimation—that has called men and women for as long as we can remember and will continue to call after we have passed.

—Edward F. Stanton

Community and Peace

Without those other pilgrims...what an empty experience this solitude would have been; for they and others too have given this journey greater depth and significance. And from these people and from the peace of walking and singing and painting alone, has come a deep sense of well-being.

—Mark Hoare

The Camino as a Springboard

If the journey meant anything, it meant that the last steps into Santiago were the first steps of another journey...You realized that the road to Compostela is a beginning, not an end.

—Laurie Dennett

Prime

Soggy Sauntering

Walking is a little fun today in the cold rain.

—Joan Myers

Glimpsing Ents

It was a gray, chilly day, absolutely perfect for

hiking. There was no rain, and the clouds were high enough that the view of the distant hills was clear, and there was plenty of light....There were small farm holdings, and a great walking track like a bridle path, wide, flat, soft underfoot. We walked through magical woods...with huge, old tree trunks looking like frozen wood spirits.

—*Sophronia Camp*

The Shadow Knows

There's something about the experience on foot that seems to sharpen or even change the perception, something that's undoubtedly induced in part by its great length and difficulty. I've seen many beautiful sunrises, but none like those I experienced along the trails in Spain in the early morning, with the rising sun right behind me and my long-shadow pointing straight, exactly straight, ahead like some mystical sign indicating the way, directly west.

—*Conrad Rudolph*

Terce

Powerful Pilgrim

Running on pure pilgrim power I stumbled on.

—*Tim Moore*

The Camino Finally Revealed

These two days were filled with grace and blessing. I felt on a different plane of the camino, a plunge into the deeply spiritual. Of course, the physical was always right there, as well—but faded somehow. I felt so alive to this other, and it came right on the heels of a sort of downtime of looking toward the end of the journey. Now a whole new layer of the camino revealed itself.

—*Sophronia Camp*

Appreciating the Cultural Landscape

Now...we began to descend through a landscape of lurid, rustic abundance, the greenometer turned up to eleven. Fields divided not with fences but paleolithic slabs of slate, a woman chasing a horse round her farmyard, an old Escort with a hay-bale in its boot, a proud family in their Saturday best off to market in the back of their tractor trailer.

—*Tim Moore*

Sext

Extreme Beauty

How strange this is, how fearsomely beautiful.

—*Kathryn Harrison*

Serenading a Forest

As the last of the morning mist dispersed, slanting bars of light played over the smooth grey trunks and the umber carpeting of last autumn's leaves. I strode along, singing.

—*Laurie Dennett*

Pathway to Lucidity

Walking with simplicity, meant that ones's mind was clear, open and receptive.

—*Judy Foot*

None

Chocolate's Wonderful Effect

I got a real charge after lunch and started to zoom for a five-kilometer stretch—walking sticks flying…. I was totally wiped at the end of my spurt, but these bursts of energy, which I attributed mostly to chocolate, were exhilarating.

Since I was so often lagging, whenever I felt a rush, I loved to go with it as I knew it wouldn't last.

—Sophronia Camp

Pine Soul and the Lessons of Pain

Somewhat recovered we started the descent. In the distance we could see forests and hills; on either side of our road were pine trees. The air was filled with the fresh green scent of evergreens. Despite the pain, despite the exhaustion, I was glad to be walking. Inside a car, I would have missed the wild flowers, the pine-rich air, the accomplishment, and the lessons of pain.

—Ellen O. Feinberg

The Bearable Lightness of Being

I took off my pack. Without the weight on my back I floated, disconnected from the ground.

—Maria & Donald Schell

Vespers

Suffering's Joy

Even my restless nights in dormitory bunks seemed somehow appropriate, for they had added

the element of sackcloth and ashes to what might
otherwise have been too comfortable a time. I
had struggled, but I was richly rewarded for my
pains....[I] felt a tremendous sense of satisfac-
tion, even joy.

—Anne Mustoe

The Camino's Palette

Late afternoon is the best time, when one steps
out of the shadow of a mountain or a cloud and
suddenly the sun is strong on the slopes, yellow-
brown with a tinge of faded green, and then
imperceptibly the glory fades, and the air grows
darker, and colours merge into one, and night
comes.

—Andrea Kirby

Relishing the Comforts of Ritual

Unaccountably, the idea of Mass in a cathedral
is a catalyst for tears; perhaps it's the idea of
shelter, the smell of the incense, candle flames.

—Kathryn Harrison

Compline

The Benefits of Exploration

I began to explore during the walk those elements that are often hidden from consciousness amidst the business of everyday life.

—David Gibson

Tallying the Balance Sheet

But it was all worth it, every last wincing movement, every lost nerve ending, every drop of sweat, every meal of bread and water.

—Conrad Rudolph

Road Scholar

Whatever the road had to teach could be apprehended by anyone—anyone whose spirit was open to learn, that is. And more than that, its lessons confirm a great truth that many of us have known all along: that we are entirely separate neither one from another, nor from the rest of creation, nor from the past and those whose lives were of the past.

—Laurie Dennett

STAGE
THE THIRTEENTH

Lauds

A Gift of the Camino

Perhaps this was really the Camino's gift. Life didn't change, but perspectives did.

—*Kerry Egan*

Sweet Sorrow

The end of a journey is always a parting of lovers.

—*Andrea Kirby*

The Tunnel's Light in Sight

This was the day we had been looking forward to. It was the final day in our long journey.

—*Bob Tuggle*

Prime

Surreal Moments

It was the peacefulness and pleasure in these little stops that was so striking....There was no urgency, no hurry. I did feel truly "in the moment" out here. Some of it had to do with the heat, I'm sure. There was a breathless, motionless quality—a kind of surrealism, as if everything was in the sharpest focus and also slow in motion.

—*Sophronia Camp*

The Beckoning Horizon

Now my body seemed to walk itself, the road walking my body. I realized that I could go on walking around the world if only the land did not end.

—*Edward F. Stanton*

Faith

We spent the whole afternoon chatting: the people we'd met, the things we'd seen, the places nobody should miss, the endless surprises of being on the way. All three were aglow with faith in human nature.

—*Ben Nimmo*

Terce

Return of the Kinglet

It was a splendid day to be a pilgrim abroad: after long weeks of thick, unventilated heat and a short day of savage precipitation, the laundered air was sweet and bracing. The prospects verdant and rollingly fecund. Dewdrops winked in the sun, sleek livestock graciously browsed lustrous pastures. I felt like a happy hobbit coming home.

—Tim Moore

The Comfort of the Multitudes

There was something comforting standing on that hill, in realizing that we were not the only people to be thirsty and discouraged, in realizing that millions of people had walked this way before, with the same goal, perhaps even the same doubts.

—Kerry Egan

The End of the Beginning

We set out and we return. And we set out / for something which never has been reached, because to do so is to go beyond it, / and we return / to something within us which has never come into

being / nor passed away. / All other offers of
certainly are as evasive / as those small / flur-
ries and scatters of birds that keep drifting on /
just ahead of you / down the whole length of a
hedgerow when you are / out there walking.

—Neil Curry

Sext

Drowning in Landscape

After all that two-dimensional trudge, there
was now much too much landscape. Epic
prospects opened up on all sides, undulating,
rain-fed fertility receding into a distant distance.

—Tim Moore

Internal Weather Report

That...morning it was raining. But there was
sunshine in my heart. I was about to arrive at
Santiago de Compostela.

—David Gibson

Solitude at the End of the World

On we went, and made four of the last seven
kilometers quite easily in forty-five minutes
along the loveliest kind of road and landscape—

absolutely alone, at the end of the world.

—*Sophronia Camp*

None

Making Magnificent Mileage

I took to the road again. It spiraled down from the high ridge above. There were cuckoos calling and larks singing, banks of white cistus rose and drifts of ivory bloom. The clouds rolled away, the sun appeared, and the air was sweet-scented and warm. It was a magnificent afternoon to walk the Camino.

—*Nicholas Luard*

Deep Immersion

This may have been the loveliest afternoon of the whole trip—a walk through old, old woods on a very soft path and through a little valley. We crossed over a stream and found the perfect spot for a foot soak that turned into a skinny dip for me, because the water was just irresistibly clear and cold and there was a sand bottom.

—*Sophronia Camp*

The Best Kind of Ache

My legs ached to bound down that invitingly sinuous descent with elastic, whistle-accompanied strides.

—Tim Moore

Vespers

Soulful Reflections

I think I understood what the ancient pilgrims must have felt at that moment. Exhaustion pushed down on me like a leaden blanket, and my body ached with every step. But when I saw that steeple, my faith lifted my soul within me, even as my body sank with weariness.

—Karen Whitehill

The Humility of Goal Achievement

I had often wondered how I would feel when I actually arrived. I don't think that I had in fact anticipated the feeling of quiet, calm and peace. It was a satisfactory conclusion to all that had gone on before. After all, I thought, I had only walked.

—Judy Foot

Walters' Wise Words

And now in the fullness of my age I had followed the road once more in an attempt to gather up the memories of a lifetime. As I sat meditating in the silent chapel, the murmur of the crowds of pilgrims in the cathedral and outside in the streets came to me like the gentle roll of the ocean tide, and I repeated to myself the lines of Sir Walter Raleigh:

> Give me my scallop-shell of quiet,
> My staff of faith to walk upon,
> My scrip of joy, immortal diet,
> My bottle of salvation,
> My gown of glory, hope's true gage,
> And thus I'll take my pilgrimage.

—Walter Starkie

Compline

The Road Goes Ever On and On

Our Camino continues, daily walking, daily discoveries of gratitude, daily surprises, not all of them joyful, and the reminder to keep on.

—Maria & Donald Schell

Around the Corner There May Wait...

The journey will continue through a thousand stops and starts, half-successes, doubts, failures and surprises. Though the future is uncertain, the present is not. This month, these days, this moment will always shine out among the ashes of my life, full of grace and freedom.

—*Edward F. Stanton*

In the Context of Time

I also knew that for me, my walk was not over, it had only begun. I would need time for reflection and resolution. I would need to share the treasures that I had found and maybe someday I would need to return to the Camino.

—*Judy Foot*

References

Brierley, J. 2003. *A Pilgrim's Guide to the Camino Francés.* Camino Guides.

Frey, N.L. 1998. *Pilgrim Stories: On and Off the Road to Santiago.* Univ. California Press.

Jacobs, M. 2002. *The Road to Santiago.* Pallas Athene.

Lozono, M.B. 2004. *A Practical Guide for Pilgrims: The Road to Santiago de Compostela.* Everest.

Melezer, W. 1993. *The pilgrims' guide to Santiago de Compostela.* Italica Press.

Polyphonia Antigua. 1990. *Ultreia! Sur la Route de Saint-Jacques de-Compostelle.* Music CD.

Raju, A. 2003. *The Way of St. James: Le Puy to the Pyrenees.* Cicerone.

Rogers, R. 2006. *Books of Hours in the Wellesley College Library*. www.wellesley.edu/

Roux, J. (and others). 2004. *The Roads to Santiago de Compostela*. MSM In Situ Themes.

Starkie, W. 1957. *The Road to Santiago: Pilgrims of St. James*. E.P. Dutton and Co., Inc.

Sumption, J. 2003. *The Age of Pilgrimage: The Medieval Journey to God*. HiddenSpring.

QUOTATION SOURCES

Buck, Jean Ann. 2004. *Walking for Wildlife: El Camino to Santiago de Compostela*. Upfront Publ.

Camp, Sophronia. 2002. *A Pilgrim's Journal: Walking El Camino de Santiago*. Sophronia Camp Publ.

Clem, Jim and Eleanor. 2004. *Buen Camino*. Page-Free Publishing Inc.

Curry, Neil. 1992. *Walking to Santiago*. Enitharmon.

Dennett, Laurie. 1987. *A Hug for the Apostle: On Foot from Chartres to Santiago de Compostela*. Canada Publ. Corp.

Egan, Kerry. 2004. *Fumbling: A Pilgrimage Tale of Love, Grief, and Spiritual Renewal on the Camino de Santiago.* Random House Inc.

Feinberg, Ellen O. 1989. *Following the Milky Way: A Pilgrimage Across Spain.* Iowa State Univ. Press.

Foot, Judy. 1997. *Foot by Foot to Santiago de Compostela.* Judy Foot Publ.

Gibson, David. 2002. *Walking in My Shadow.* Guildhall Press.

Harrison, Kathryn. 2003. *The Road to Santiago.* National Geographic Society.

Hanbury-Tenison, Robin. 1990. *Spanish Pilgrimage: A Canter to St. James.* Long Rider's Guild Press.

Hitt, Jack. 2005. *Off the Road: A Modern-day Walk Down the Pilgrim's Route into Spain.* Simon & Schuster Inc.

Hoare, Mark. 2003. *A Painting Pilgrim: A Journey to Santiago de Compostela.* Mudwall Press.

Hoinacki, Lee. 1997. *El Camino: Walking to Santiago de Compostela.* Pennsylvania State Univ. Press.

Kenney, Sue. 2004. *Sue Kenney's My Camino.* White Knight Publications.

Kirby, Andrea. 1996. *Andrea Kirby's Walk on El Camino*. www.jrnet.com/travel/articles/santiago.html.

Lasswell, Linda L. 2005. *Walking Home on the Camino de Santiago*. Pilgrims Process Inc.

Luard, Nicholas. 1998. *The Field of the Star: A Pilgrim's Journey to Santiago de Compostela*. Michael Joseph Ltd.

MacLaine, Shirley. 2000. *The Camino: A Journey of the Spirit*. Simon & Schuster Inc.

Moore, Tim. 2004. *Travels with My Donkey: One Man and His Ass on a Pilgrimage to Santiago*. St. Martin's Press.

Mullins, Edwin. 2001. *The Pilgrimage to Santiago*. Interlink Books.

Mustoe, Anne. 2005. *Amber, Furs and Cockleshells: Bike Rides with Pilgrims and Merchants*. Virgin Books.

Myers, Joan. 1991. *Santiago: Saint of Two Worlds*. Univ. of New Mexico Press.

Neillands, Rob. 1985. *The Road to Compostela*. Moorland Publ.

Nelson, Howard. 1998. *Trust and Tears: Poems of Pilgrimage*. Copyprints Ltd.

Nimmo, Ben. 2001. *Pilgrim Snail: Busking to Santiago*. Ulvercroft Foundation.

Poë, Emma. 2000. *Diary of a Pilgrim*. E. Poë Publ.

Robberstad, Knud Helge. 1996. *The Road to Santiago: A Journey to Santiago de Compostela*. Verbum Grafiske Stavanger.

Rudolph, Conrad. 2004. *Pilgrimage to the End of the World: The Road to Santiago de Compostela*. Univ. of Chicago Press.

Schell, Maria and Donald. 2001. *My Father, My Daughter*. Church Publ. Inc.

Selby, Bettina. 1994. *Pilgrim's Road: A Journey to Santiago de Compostela*. Little, Brown and Company.

Slader, Bert. 1986. *Pilgrim's Footsteps: A Walk Along the Ancient Road to Santiago de Compostela*. Quest Books.

Stanton, Edward F. 1994. *Road of Stars to Santiago*. Univ. Press of Kentucky.

Starkie, Walter. 1954. *The Road to Santiago: Pilgrims of St. James*. E.P. Dutton and Company.

Tuggle, Bob. 2000. *On the Road to Santiago*. Writers Club Press.

Wallis, Mary Victoria. 2003. *Among the Pilgrims: Journeys to Santiago de Compostela*. Trafford.

Watson, Christabel. 2005. *A Walk From Gibraltar to la Coruna*. Newbold-on-Stour.

Whitehill, Karen. 1990. *A Walk Across Holy Ground*. Tyndale House Publ.

IMAGE
SOURCES

Front cover: print of *The Jakobsbrüder* by Josh
Amman, 1568; from Hoinacki (1997); original from
Bayerische Staatsbibliothek, to whom I communi-
cated for permission.

Other Medieval prints: photographed from pilgrim
information boards along the Chemin de Saint
Jacques in the Lazère on the Le Puy route.

Modern pilgrim insignia: photographed from the
restaurant *La Locanda del Pellegrino* on Via del
Pelligrino in the traditional pilgrim quarter near
Campo del Fiori in Rome.

About The Editor

ROBERT LAWRENCE FRANCE is a professor at the Harvard University Design School where he teaches courses on ecological management and environmental theory and conducts research on cultural landscapes such as the Camino de Santiago. He has authored numerous technical papers and many books including *Deep Immersion: The Experience of Water*, as well as being the editor of two previous books of complied quotations: *Profitably Soaked: Thoreau's Engagement with Water* and *Wetlands of Mass Destruction: Ancient Presage for Contemporary Ecocide in Southern Iraq*, all published by Green Frigate Books. Dr. France has undertaken many long-distance walks around the world including the Way of Saint James and, most notably, a three-month crossing of Ellesmere

Island, the longest man-haul sledging journey in the Canadian High Arctic since the days of the Franklin search.

ABOUT THE FOREWORD WRITER

MATTHEW FOX is author of over two dozen books, including *Original Blessing, The Reinvention of Work, Creativity: Where the Divine and the Human Meet, One River, Many Wells: Wisdom Springing from Global Faiths, A Spirituality Named Compassion,* his most recent, *A New Reformation!,* and the forthcoming *The A.W.E. Project: An Educational Transformation for Post-Modern Times.* Fox's books have received numerous awards and he is the recipient of the Peace Abbey Courage of Conscience Award, of which other recipients have included the Dalai Lama, Mother Teresa and Rosa Parks. The noted theologian Thomas Berry has written that "Matthew Fox might well be the most creative, the most comprehensive, surely the most challenging religious-spiritual teacher in America. He has the scholarship, the imagination, the courage, the writing skill to fulfill this role at a time when the more official Christian theological traditions are having difficulty in establishing any vital contact with own most creative spiritual traditions of the past… He has, it seems, created a new mythic context for leading us out of our contemporary religious and spiritual confusion into a new clarity of mind and peace of soul, by affirming rather than abandoning any of our traditional beliefs." For more information, see www.MatthewFox.org.

Further Readings
on the Way of St. James
by Robert France

Look for the following titles currently in preparation for
publication over the next several years

Star Struck: The Experience of the
Compostela Pilgrimage
—comprehensive and critical literature review—

Godspeed: France by Foot on
Pilgrimage Toward Compostela
—journal account of the four French routes—

Going Over Old Ground: Walking to and
From the Ends of the World on Pilgrimage
to Santiago, Ellesmere, and Beyond
—review of long-distance walks around the world—

Along the Way: Reflections on the
Camino Francès/France's Road
—namesake road as life metaphor—

OTHER GREEN FRIGATE BOOKS

*Healing Natures, Repairing Relationships: New Perspectives on
Restoring Ecological Spaces and Consciousness*
Robert L. France

Where We Live: Chasing the Dream of Urban Sustainability
Robert M. Abbott and Mark Holland

GREEN FRIGATE BOOKS

"THERE IS NO FRIGATE LIKE A BOOK"

Words on the page have the power to transport us, and in the process, transform us. Such journeys can be far reaching, traversing the landscapes of the external world and that within, as well as the timescapes of the past, present and future.

Green Frigate Books is a small publishing house offering a vehicle—a ship—for those seeking to conceptually sail and explore the horizons of the natural and built environments, and the relations of humans within them. Our goal is to reach an educated lay readership by producing works that fall in the cracks between those offered by traditional academic and popular presses.